COOKING WITH STONE GROUND FLOUR

by

Arlene Kovash
and
Marcie Anderson

THE BOOK MILL
32855 PEORIA ROAD
CORVALLIS, OREGON 97330

ADD A NEW DIMENSION TO YOUR COOKING EXPERIENCE WITH STONE GROUND FLOUR

Published by: The Book Mill
Illustrations by: Dorothy Hagerty

ISBN 0-9605394-1-7

CONTENTS

INTRODUCTION

Marcie Anderson learned to cook on her grandparents' homestead in Oregon's Willamette Valley. Grandma Dietz taught her the joy of gathering, preparing and cooking with the natural ingredients available: honey, berries, vegetables, fruits and stone ground flour.

After receiving her bachelor's degree from Oregon State University, Marcie eventually settled with her family on a farm near Corvallis. There, her children prodded her into reviving her recipes and developing new ones. Sons, Daryl and Ron brought in freshly harvested wheat from the combine. The wheat was cleaned and ground for Saturday's "baking day" where daughter Lynn joined in.

Arlene Kovash's cooking experience came from her home economics training at Arizona and Oregon State Universities and from her 20 years of experience as a 4-H member and leader. Her daughters Lorraine and Suzanne have also become competent cooks, assisting with bread baking and meal preparation on the family farm.

As long time friends, Marcie and Arlene decided to combine their stone ground flour recipes and publish a cookbook. They are grateful to Reed and Maryana Vollstedt for their encouragement and consultation in the writing of this book.

4

ON USING STONE GROUND FLOUR

To substitute stone ground flour for white all-purpose flour in your recipes:

FOR : 1 cup white all-purpose flour

USE : 7/8 cup stone ground flour

The first few times you convert your white flour recipes, a good rule is to replace only half the white flour with stone ground flour, then gradually work up to using all stone ground flour if you wish.

Stone ground flour absorbs moisture more slowly than white flour. Add stone ground flour first, mix well, then add any white flour required.

In bread recipes dough may still be slightly sticky when enough flour is added. To test — let dough rest a few minutes. It will retain its shape when enough flour has been added.

To keep stone ground flour fresh and nutritious, cover tightly and store in the refrigerator or freezer.

July 00

ON USING HONEY

To substitute honey for sugar in a recipe, use as little as 1/2 cup honey for 1 cup sugar and slightly reduce the liquid in the recipe.

RAISING YEAST DOUGH

To raise dough, find a draft-free place with a temperature of about 85-90° F:

The pilot light in a gas oven warms it to an ideal temperature. Use caution in putting the dough into a slightly heated electric oven. It is easy to get the oven too warm. Check the temperature with a small oven thermometer.

Turn the dough out onto a slightly oiled board and set your mixing bowl upside down over the dough for the first raising. The bowl traps the moist warmth of the dough.

The top of a waterheater is often good.

Run some hot water into the sink and set the bowl of dough in it.

If you have a microwave oven, boil a cup of water for several minutes to warm the interior of the oven. Push the water into a corner of the oven and place the dough inside.

If the dough doesn't seem to be raising as high as you'd like in the pan, check your pan size. It is especially important to have the correct pan size for whole wheat bread, usually 8½".

REASONS FOR BREAD BAKING
DISAPPOINTMENTS:

Bread will be dry and crumbly if too much flour has been added, or if flour has been added late in the kneading process.

The dough will not rise if the temperature of the water for dissolving the yeast is either too cold or too hot, if the dough is too stiff, if the place for rising is too cool, or if the yeast is too old.

Too warm of rising place will weaken or kill the yeast so that the bread will either not rise, or will rise and fall.

If dough raises too fast or too long, bread will be coarse or may fall.

Refer to bread baking tips throughout the yeast bread section.

6

APPETIZERS

SESAME SEED CRACKERS

Serve these with a dip or cheese crackers.

1 cup stone ground flour
1/2 tsp. salt
1/2 cup sesame seeds

1/3 cup butter

2 Tbsp. cold water

Stir together flour, salt, sesame seeds. Cut in butter. Sprinkle water over mixture and stir lightly until evenly moistened and dough forms a ball. Add a few more drops of water if needed.

On lightly floured surface roll dough out to about 1/8 inch thickness. Using a pastry or pizza cutter and a ruler cut dough into 1 1/2 inch strips. Cut the other direction to form squares or diamonds. Place on greased cookie sheet. Bake 15-20 minutes at 325°.

TANGY CHEESE WAFERS

1 jar (5 oz.) sharp cheese spread
1/4 cup soft butter or margarine
2/3 cup stone ground flour
5-10 drops Tabasco sauce
2 Tbsp. sesame seeds or finely ground nuts

Beat together first 4 ingredients until smooth. Shape into 12" roll. Roll in sesame seeds or finely ground nuts. Wrap and chill until firm. Cut into 1/4" slices and bake 10 minutes at 400°. Serve warm or cold.

Roll may be frozen until needed. Thaw before slicing.

QUICK BREADS

GOLDEN PUMPKIN BREAD

Pumpkin and stone ground flour are naturals together!

1 cup cooked pumpkin
1 cup sugar
1/2 cup milk
2 eggs

2 cups stone ground flour
2 tsp. baking powder
1/2 tsp. soda
1 tsp. salt
1 1/2 tsp. pumpkin pie spice

1/4 cup softened margarine
1 cup chopped nuts

Combine pumpkin, sugar, milk and eggs in mixing bowl. Stir together dry ingredients and add to pumpkin mixture. Beat in margarine. Stir in nuts.

Spoon into well-greased 9½" loaf pan or three 3" x 5½" loaf pans. Bake 50 minutes at 350° for 9" pan and 40 minutes for 5" pans, or until toothpick inserted in center comes out clean. Cool in pan 5-10 minutes. This bread freezes well.

8

ORANGE BREAD

1 1/2 cups stone ground flour
1 1/2 cups all-purpose flour
1 cup sugar
1 Tbsp. baking powder
1 tsp. salt

3/4 cup Grape-Nuts cereal

1/4 cup margarine, melted
3/4 cup orange juice
3/4 cup milk
1 Tbsp. orange rind
1 egg, beaten

Measure flours, sugar, baking powder and salt into a large mixing bowl. Stir through with a fork to blend. Stir in Grape-Nuts cereal.

Stir margarine, orange juice, milk and orange rind into egg. Stir liquid ingredients into dry ingredients. Blend until all flour is moistened.

Spoon batter into a greased 9½" loaf pan. Bake at 350° for 1 hour. Cool in pan 10 minutes. Remove from pan and finish cooling on cake rack.

To substitute honey for sugar in a recipe, use as little as 1/2 cup honey for 1 cup sugar and slightly reduce the liquid in the recipe.

BRAN MUFFINS

1 1/4 cups stone ground flour
1/2 tsp. salt
1 1/4 tsp. soda

1 1/2 cups all-bran cereal
1/2 cup boiling water

1 egg, slightly beaten
1 cup buttermilk
1/2 cup honey
1/4 cup margarine, melted

1 cup raisins or chopped dates or chopped prunes

Measure first 3 ingredients into a mixing bowl and mix well with a fork.

Pour boiling water over bran cereal, stir and cool to lukewarm. Add egg, buttermilk, honey, margarine and raisins. Stir until well blended. Add dry ingredients and stir just until evenly moistened.

Fill greased muffin tins 3/4 full. Bake 20-25 minutes at 425°. Makes 18 muffins.

If stone ground whole wheat flour is unavailable, whole wheat flour produced commercially may be substituted; however, the unique texture and flavor will not be as robust. The purchase of the best stone ground flour available will reward your time and effort.

BLUEBERRY MUFFINS

2 cups stone ground flour
1/2 tsp. salt
1/2 cup sugar
1 Tbsp. baking powder

2 eggs
1/4 cup margarine, melted
1 cup plain yogurt

2 cups blueberries

Measure dry ingredients into a large bowl. Stir with a fork to blend.

Beat eggs lightly. Beat in margarine and yogurt. Stir egg mixture into dry ingredients. Gently fold in blueberries.

Fill greased muffin tins 3/4 full. Bake 20-25 minutes at 400°. Makes 18 muffins.

COTTAGE CHEESE MUFFINS

You will enjoy the fresh taste the lemon peel gives to these muffins.

1 cup stone ground flour
3/4 cup all-purpose flour
1 Tbsp. baking powder
1/4 tsp. salt

1/4 cup soft margarine
1/3 cup sugar
1/2 cup cream-style cottage cheese
1 tsp. grated lemon peel
1 egg
1/2 cup milk

Measure dry ingredients into a bowl and stir with a fork to blend.

In mixer bowl, cream margarine and sugar. Beat in cottage cheese and lemon peel. Add egg and milk and beat well. Stir in dry ingredients just until moistened.

Fill greased muffin tins 3/4 full. Bake 20-25 minutes at 400°. Makes 18 muffins.

PANCAKES

Pancakes made with stone ground flour have a pleasant, nutty flavor -- not as doughy as an ordinary pancake.

2 cups stone ground flour
1 Tbsp. sugar
1 tsp. salt
1 1/2 tsp. soda
1 tsp. baking powder

2 eggs
1 1/2 cups buttermilk
1/2 cup water
1/3 cup cooking oil

Measure dry ingredients into bowl. Stir together with a fork to blend. Stir together liquid ingredients and add to dry mixture, stirring only until moistened. Bake on hot griddle.

For pancake mix: Mix up 4 or 5 times the amount of dry ingredients and store in an airtight container. When ready to serve, measure out 2 cups of the mix and add the liquid ingredients.

WAFFLES

The combination of fresh stone ground flour and yogurt makes these waffles extra special.

3 eggs
1 cup milk
1/2 cup plain yogurt or buttermilk

2 cups stone ground flour
3 tsp. baking powder
1/2 tsp. soda
1/2 tsp. salt
1 Tbsp. sugar

1/2 cup margarine, melted

In mixer bowl, beat eggs until light and lemon colored. Mix in milk and yogurt.

Stir together dry ingredients. Add to egg mixture and blend well. Stir in melted margarine. Bake in hot waffle iron. Makes eight 6" waffles.

APPLESAUCE-NUT COFFEECAKE

Applesauce, stoneground flour, spices and nuts blend together for a delightful treat. Great to serve to a group.

1 1/4 cups applesauce
1 cup sugar
1/2 cup cooking oil
2 eggs
1/4 cup milk

2 cups stone ground flour
1 tsp. soda
1/2 tsp. each salt, baking powder, cinnamon, nutmeg
   and allspice
3/4 cup ground nuts

Mix together applesauce, sugar, oil, eggs and milk. Beat in remaining ingredients. Pour into greased and floured 8" x 12" pan. Combine topping ingredients and sprinkle over batter. Bake for 40-45 minutes at 350°. Serve warm or cold.

Topping: 1/2 cup each ground nuts and brown sugar
          1 tsp. cinnamon

Double the recipe. Serve one warm from the oven and freeze the other to reheat when friends drop in or to give as a gift.

Buttermilk, yogurt, and sour cream may be interchanged in most recipes. One cup buttermilk = one cup plain yogurt = one cup sour cream.

JAZZED-UP IRISH SODA BREAD

When Sally Goodwin was a student at OSU, she developed this version of Irish Soda Bread. It soon became a favorite of her friends on campus.

1 1/2 cups stone ground flour
1 1/2 cups -- your choice: oatmeal, wheat germ, corn meal,
   soy flour, etc.
1 tsp. soda
1/2 tsp. salt

1 cup buttermilk or milk
1 egg, beaten
1 Tbsp. honey or molasses or brown sugar

Mix dry ingredients together. Add wet ingredients. (Dough should be dry enough to knead.) Knead a few minutes, then shape into a round, flat loaf about the size of your hand.

Dust loaf with flour on all sides. With sharp knife, cut 3 parallel slits in top of loaf so it won't crack. Place on greased cookie sheet and bake 25 minutes at 375º.

Sally says, "It holds together nicely even when sliced thin. Makes especially good toast. (Spread butter and honey on toast, then broil -- m-m-m!) My favorite sandwich: Cover two slices bread with Swiss or Cheddar cheese, broil, put a gob of sprouts between the two and munch out!"

BUTTERMILK CORNBREAD

This is a lighter textured and more moist cornbread than the usual. Easy to mix by hand.

2 eggs
1/4 cup sugar
1 cup buttermilk

1 cup stone ground flour
2/3 cup cornmeal
2 tsp. baking powder
1/4 tsp. soda
1/2 tsp. salt

1/4 cup butter or margarine, melted

Beat eggs well. Add sugar. Stir in buttermilk. Stir together dry ingredients and add to egg mixture, mixing well. Stir in melted butter or margarine and pour into greased 8" square baking dish. Bake for 25 minutes at 400°. Serve hot.

BAKING POWDER BISCUITS

1 7/8 cups stone ground flour
3/4 tsp. salt
3 tsp. baking powder

1/3 cup butter, margarine or shortening

2/3 cup milk

Measure dry ingredients into a bowl and stir to blend. Cut in butter, margarine or shortening. Add milk all at once and stir with a fork until all ingredients are moistened.

Turn out onto a lightly floured pastry cloth or board. Gently knead 8 or 10 times, or until dough is smooth and no longer sticky. Roll or pat to about 3/8" thick. Cut with a floured cutter, or cut into squares with a sharp knife. Place on ungreased cookie sheet and bake 15 minutes at 425°. Makes 12 or more biscuits.

ORANGE POTATO DOUGHNUTS

2 cups soft mashed potatoes -- instant may be used

3 eggs
1 1/4 cups sugar
1/2 Tbsp. grated orange peel
1 tsp. vanilla

4 1/2 cups stone ground flour
2 Tbsp. baking powder
1 1/2 tsp. salt
1 tsp. nutmeg OR mace

3/4 cup sugar
Grated rind of 1 orange

Chill mashed potatoes.

Beat eggs in mixer till light. Add chilled mashed potatoes, sugar, grated orange peel and vanilla and beat well.

Stir dry ingredients together and add to potato mixture to make a soft dough. Chill well.

Roll 1/3 of dough at a time to 1/2" thickness on a floured pastry cloth or board. Cut with floured doughnut cutter. Fry in deep fat at 365°-375°, 1 1/2 minutes on each side. Drain. Dip in a mixture of 3/4 cup sugar and grated rind of 1 orange. Makes about 3 dozen.

No doughnut cutter? Use a 2 1/2" biscuit cutter and cut out the centers with any shape 1" cutter, or cut the center out in a triangle shape with a sharp knife. The hole helps the doughnut cook all the way through.

YEAST BREADS

BASIC 100% STONE GROUND WHEAT FLOUR

1 Tbsp. brown sugar
2 1/4 cups warm water
2 packages dry yeast

6-7 cups stone ground flour
3/4 cup dry powdered milk
1/2 cup brown sugar
2 tsp. salt
1/3 cup cooking oil

Dissolve 1 Tbsp. brown sugar in the water and add yeast. Combine 5 cups flour, powdered milk, 1/2 cup brown sugar and salt. Stir in yeast mixture and oil. Stir in enough of the remaining flour to make a soft dough.

Knead until smooth. Let rise until double, about 1 hour. Punch down, divide and form into 2 loaves. Place in well-greased 8½" bread pans. Let rise until almost the shape desired, 45 minutes to an hour. Bake 15 minutes at 400°; reduce temperature to 350° and bake 30 minutes more.

A candy thermometer can be a big help to the beginning baker. Check the temperature of liquids until you develop a feel for "warm" and "lukewarm." Yeast needs to be dissolved in a "warm" liquid: 105°-115° F. Often other liquid ingredients are to be "lukewarm:" 95°-105° F.

SANDWICH BREAD

A basic recipe using part stone ground flour and part white flour.

Vary the amount of stone ground flour according to taste.

1/2 cup milk
3 Tbsp. sugar
2 tsp. salt
3 Tbsp. margarine or oil

1 package dry yeast
1 1/2 cups warm water
3 cups stone ground flour
3 - 3 1/2 cups white all-purpose flour or bread flour

Scald milk and pour over sugar, salt and margarine in large bowl. Cool to lukewarm.

Dissolve yeast in warm water. Add it with the stone ground flour and 1 cup all-purpose flour to milk mixture. Beat until smooth, 2 minutes by hand or mixer. Gradually add enough of the remaining flour to make a moderately soft dough.

Knead by hand or bread mixer until smooth and elastic, about 7 minutes. Place in lightly greased bowl; turn once to grease top. Cover and let rise 1 hour.

Punch down and let rise 1/2 hour more. Shape into 2 loaves and let rise in well-greased 8 1/2" loaf pans until almost the shape desired, 45 minutes to 1 hour. Bake 30 minutes at 375°. Remove from pans immediately and cool on racks.

For a faster raising lighter loaf of bread, increase the amount of yeast to 1/2 again as much as called for. For 1 package, use 1 1/2 packages; for 2 packages, use 3.

BUTTERMILK CRACKED WHEAT BREAD

Buttermilk and honey make this a moist, flavorful loaf.

2 packages dry yeast
1/2 cup warm water

2 cups buttermilk
2 Tbsp. cooking oil
1/4 cup honey
1 Tbsp. salt

1/2 tsp. soda
1 cup cracked wheat
5 1/2 - 6 cups stone ground flour

Soften yeast in water. Combine the buttermilk, oil, honey and salt and heat to lukewarm. Add to yeast mixture.

Stir in soda, cracked wheat and 3 cups stone ground flour. Beat in enough of the remaining flour to make a soft dough.

Knead until smooth and elastic, about 5-10 minutes. Let rise until double, about one hour. Punch down, divide in 2 and form into loaves. Place in well-greased 8½" pans. Let rise until almost the shape desired, about 45 minutes. Bake 35 minutes at 375°.

This loaf is also very good without cracked wheat; increase flour to 6 1/2 - 7 cups.

To prevent the top of the loaf from becoming too brown, make a tent of foil and lay over bread during last half of baking.

19

MINIATURE LOAVES

Company coming for lunch? Greet them with the aroma of freshly baked loaves, or reheated loaves from the freezer. Set a tureen of soup on the table. Put a loaf of bread on a small cutting board at each place. A cheese tray and bowl of apples and pears complete the menu.

2 cups milk
1/4 cup margarine

1/3 cup honey

2 packages dry yeast
1 tsp. honey
2/3 cup warm water

6·1/2 · 7 cups stone ground flour
2 tsp. salt

Heat milk and margarine together just until margarine is melted. Stir in honey. Cool to lukewarm.

Dissolve yeast and 1 tsp. honey in warm water. Place 3 cups of the flour in a large bowl. Stir in salt. Add milk mixture and yeast. Stir well with a wooden spoon. Gradually add enough of the remaining flour to make a firm dough.

Turn dough out onto a floured board and knead 10 minutes or until dough is smooth and elastic. Place in a greased bowl, turning once to grease top. Cover and put in a warm place until doubled in bulk, about 1 hour.

Punch dough down and divide into 6 equal pieces. Shape into loaves and place in well-greased 3" x 5½" loaf pans. Cover and let rise until doubled, about 30 minutes. Place pans on a cookie sheet. Bake 25-30 minutes at 375º.

Dough may be divided into 8 loaves. Reduce baking time by 5 minutes.

For a soft, tender crust, brush entire loaf with butter, margarine or oil after baking.

REFRIGERATOR CRESCENT ROLLS

A no-knead dough which waits to be baked at your convenience.

2/3 cup milk
1/2 cup butter, melted
1/4 cup sugar
1/2 tsp. salt

1 package dry yeast

2 eggs, beaten
1-1/2 cups stone ground flour

1 1/2 - 2 cups all-purpose flour

Scald milk. Add butter. Stir in sugar and salt. Cool to lukewarm. Add yeast and let stand until dissolved.

Add beaten eggs and stone ground flour. Stir until thoroughly mixed. Gradually stir in enough of the all-purpose flour to make a soft dough. Place in a greased bowl, cover and refrigerate overnight.

Remove from refrigerator and let sit at room temperature 2 hours. Roll into a large circle 1/4" thick. Spread with melted butter. Cut into 16 pie-shaped wedges. Roll each wedge toward the point. Place on greased cookie sheet. Let rise until ready to bake, 1 to 6 hours. Bake 10 minutes at 400°.

For smaller rolls, divide dough into 2 balls before rolling. Cut each circle into 16 wedges.

A pizza cutter makes quick work of cutting wedges.

The exact amount of flour needed in any recipe will vary according to the area in which your wheat was grown. Add the last portion of flour called for gradually until you reach the desired consistency.

POVERTY BREAD

Our friend Pris Hardin made this bread high in protein to supplement higher cost protein sources.

3/4 cup cracked wheat
1/2 cup bran cereal
1 cup boiling water

1 egg
1 1/2 tsp. salt
1/3 cup sugar
1/4 cup melted shortening, lard, unseasoned chicken fat
   or cooking oil

1 package dry yeast
1 Tbsp. sugar
1/4 cup warm water
1 cup sourdough starter
1/2 cup warm water
1/2 cup wheat germ
1/4 cup brewer's yeast (optional)

5 1/2 −6 cups stone ground and all-purpose flour, any
   proportion

Several hours before making bread, combine cracked wheat, bran cereal and boiling water. Let cool.

Combine egg, salt, sugar and shortening. Dissolve yeast and 1 Tbsp. sugar in 1/4 cup warm water. Add the yeast, sourdough starter, 1/2 cup warm water, wheat/bran mixture, wheat germ and brewer's yeast to the egg mixture.

Add 3 cups flour and beat 2 minutes by mixer or hand. Work in 2 1/2 or more cups flour. Knead 15-20 minutes by hand, or 10 minutes with a bread mixer. Place dough in lightly greased bowl, turn once to grease top, cover and let rise until doubled, about 1 1/2 hours.

Punch down, divide and form into 2 loaves and place in well-greased 9½" bread pans. Let rise until just about the desired shape. Place in cold oven, turn to 400° and set timer for 15 minutes. After 15 minutes reduce heat to 375° and bake 25 minutes more. Remove immediately from pans and cool on racks.

SOURDOUGH BREAD

A moist bread which doesn't crumble -- ideal for lunches.

2 cups warm water
1 package dry yeast

4 cups stone ground flour
3/4 cup sourdough starter
1/3 cup dry powdered milk

1/4 cup molasses or corn syrup
1 Tbsp. salt
3 Tbsp. margarine
1 tsp. soda

3 - 3 1/2 cups all-purpose flour

Add yeast to water in large mixing bowl. Let soften 5 minutes. Stir in stone ground flour, starter and powdered milk. Beat until smooth and elastic. Cover and let stand until bubbly, about 2 hours.

Stir in molasses, salt, margarine and soda. Mix in enough of the all-purpose flour to make a stiff dough. Knead until smooth and elastic, about 10 minutes by hand or 5-7 minutes in a bread mixer. Place in lightly greased bowl, turn once to grease top, cover and let rise until double, about 1 1/2 hours.

Punch down and let rise another 1/2 hour. Shape into 2 loaves, place in well-greased 8½" bread pans and let rise until almost the shape desired, about 45 minutes. Bake 30 minutes at 375°.

If bread dough raises too fast or too long in the pan, the bread will be coarse or will fall.

If the recipe you choose calls for 9½" pans and yours are smaller, cut off half a dozen pieces of dough about the size of golf balls and make into dinner rolls.

FREDRIKA'S AUSTRIAN BREAD

Fredrika Wannemaker developed this recipe during her years of baking in her native Austria. She has a beautiful feel for baking with a variety of seeds and flours. She graciously converted "handsfull" and "servingspoons" to "cups" and "tablespoons" for us.

4 2/3 cups stone ground flour
2/3 cup wheat germ
2 Tbsp. flax seeds
2 Tbsp. sesame seeds
3 Tbsp. sunflower seeds, finely ground
1 Tbsp. caraway seeds (optional)
1 Tbsp. salt

2 packages dry yeast
1 Tbsp. sugar
1 cup warm water

1/4 cup cooking oil
1 3/4 cups lukewarm water

1 1/2 - 2 cups unbleached flour

Measure dry ingredients into a large mixing bowl. Stir to blend well.

Dissolve yeast and 1 Tbsp. sugar in warm water. Let it bubble about 15 minutes, or until almost double in bulk.

Use a wooden spoon to stir oil and water into the flour mixture. Stir in dissolved yeast. Blend in enough of the unbleached flour to make a soft dough. Knead several minutes. Set in warm place until doubled in bulk.

Punch down and knead for several minutes more. Form into 2 loaves. Place in well-greased 8 1/2" bread pans, cover and let double again.

Bake at 350° for 1 hour. Cover with foil after 20 minutes.

You may exchange up to 1 cup stone ground flour for an equal amount of buckwheat flour or rye flour. Up to 1/2 cup millet may also be exchanged.

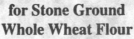

BREAD MACHINE RECIPES
for Stone Ground
Whole Wheat Flour

Stone ground whole wheat flour with its unique nutty texture and flavor works well in your bread machine.

BUTTERMILK BREAD

The buttermilk and honey help keep the bread moist.

Follow machine instructions for whole wheat flour.

Ingredients	Small Loaf	Large Loaf
buttermilk	1 cup	1 1/2 cups
butter or margarine	1 Tbsp.	1 1/2 Tbsp.
honey	1 Tbsp.	1 1/2 Tbsp.
stone ground whole wheat flour	2/3 cup	1 cup
bread flour	1 1/2 cups	2 1/4 cups
salt	3/4 tsp.	1 tsp.
active dry yeast	2 tsp.	1 Tbsp.

All ingredients must be at room temperature.
Water should be at 75°-80°.

To substitute dry buttermilk for fresh:

For	Use	Add
1 c. fresh buttermilk	1/4 c. dry buttermilk	1 c. water
1 1/2 c. fresh buttermilk	6 Tbsp. dry buttermilk	1 1/2 c. water

100% STONE GROUND FLOUR BREAD

This is our favorite bread. It is hearty with the nutrients, nutty texture and flavor of European breads.

Follow your machine instructions for order of adding ingredients.

Ingredients	Small Loaf	Large Loaf
water	1 cup	1 1/2 cups
oil	4 tsp.	2 Tbsp.
honey	4 tsp.	2 Tbsp.
stone ground whole wheat flour	2 1/4 cups	3 1/2 cups
dry milk	3 Tbsp.	1/4 cup
salt	1 tsp.	1 1/2 tsp.
active dry yeast	2 tsp.	1 Tbsp.
gluten	2 tsp.	1 Tbsp.

All ingredients must be at room temperature.
Water should be at 75°-80°.

If you want a higher, lighter American style loaf, add 1 more tablespoon of gluten.

CINNAMON RAISIN BREAD

Follow your bread machine instructions for order of adding ingredients.

Ingredients	Small Loaf	Large Loaf
buttermilk	2/3 cup	1 cup
butter or margarine	1 Tbsp.	1 1/2 Tbsp.
egg	1	1
honey	4 tsp.	2 Tbsp.
stone ground whole wheat flour	1 cup	1 1/2 cups
bread flour	1 cup	1 1/2 cups
salt	3/4 tsp.	1 tsp.
cinnamon	3/4 tsp.	1 tsp.
raisins	2/3 cup	1 cup
active dry yeast	2 tsp.	1 Tbsp.

All ingredients must be at room temperature.
Water should be at 75°-80°.

If your favorite recipe calls for bread flour only and you'd like to include stone ground flour, try replacing 1 cup bread flour with 1 cup stone ground flour. You may want to add 1 tablespoon gluten, if the loaf does not rise as high as you'd like.

Gluten is the protein which adds strength to the bread structure. It enables the heavier whole wheat breads to rise higher. Look for gluten in the flour section of your market or health food store.

HONEY OATMEAL BREAD

Honey enhances the flavor of whole wheat flour and keeps the bread moist. If you prefer molasses, substitute equal amounts.

Follow machine instructions for whole wheat flour.

Ingredients	Small Loaf	Large Loaf
water	3/4 cup	1 1/4 cup
oil	4 tsp.	2 Tbsp.
honey	4 tsp.	2 Tbsp.
stone ground whole wheat flour	2/3 cup	1 cup
bread flour	1 1/4 cups	1 3/4 cups
oats, quick or old fashioned	2/3 cup	1 cup
dry milk	3 Tbsp.	1/4 cup
salt	1 tsp.	1 1/2 tsp.
active dry yeast	2 tsp.	1 Tbsp.

All ingredients must be at room temperature.
Water should be at 75°-80°.

You may want to adjust the amount of liquids slightly in these recipes. Follow your machine instructions for whole wheat flour.

Look for yeast in 2-pound foil packages. The cost per loaf will be about 1/10 of that from the 4-oz. jars or three 1/4-oz. strip packages. For a big savings, divide a bag among friends. Store in your freezer or refrigerator in a tightly sealed package.

MAPLE-OATMEAL MIXER BREAD

1 1/4 cups milk
1/4 cup margarine
1 cup quick oatmeal

1/4 cup very warm water
1 package dry yeast
1/3 cup maple or pancake syrup

1 egg
1 1/2 tsp. salt
2 1/2 cups stone ground flour
1/2 cup cracked wheat
1/2 cup raisins

Combine milk and margarine and heat to boiling. Pour over oatmeal in mixer bowl. Cool to lukewarm. Sprinkle yeast into water; stir in 1 tsp. of the maple syrup. Let stand until double, about 15 minutes. Meanwhile, grease a 2 or 2 1/2-quart casserole and sprinkle sides and bottom with oatmeal.

Add the yeast mixture, remaining maple syrup, egg, salt and 1 1/2 cups of the flour to the oatmeal mixture. Beat with electric mixer on medium for 3 minutes. Beat in remaining flour, cracked wheat and raisins.

Spoon batter into casserole. Smooth top with wet hands. Sprinkle with 1 Tbsp. sugar mixed with 1/4 tsp. cinnamon. Let rise until double. Bake 50 minutes at 350⁰. Cool in bowl 10 minutes. Invert on rack.

If you prefer to leave out raisins or cracked wheat, increase flour to 2 3/4 cups. One-half cup chopped nuts may be added.

If the top of the bread seems to be getting too dark too fast, place a foil tent on the loaf half way through the baking time.

BASIC STONE GROUND FLOUR SWEET DOUGH

This basic dough is rich enough for tasty sweet rolls, yet makes an excellent loaf of bread or dinner rolls.

1 1/2 cups milk
2 tsp. salt
1/3 cup oil
1/3 cup honey
1/2 cup water
2 eggs
2 packages dry yeast

7 cups stone ground flour

Scald milk. Add salt, oil, honey, water, eggs and yeast in that order. (By the time the yeast is added, the milk has cooled.) Mix well. Beat in 3 cups flour and let stand 15 minutes.

Add enough flour to make a medium stiff dough. Knead 10-20 minutes, until dough is smooth and elastic. Place in lightly greased bowl, turning once to grease top. Cover and let rise until double, 45-60 minutes. Punch down and shape.

Cinnamon Rolls

Divide dough in half, rolling each to an 8" x 12" rectangle. Spread with melted butter or margarine and sprinkle with cinnamon-sugar mixture and nuts or raisins. Roll lengthwise, cut into 3/4" slices and place in greased baking pans. Let rise until doubled, about 45 minutes. Bake at 375° for 25 minutes.

Bits and Pieces

Cut dough into pieces about the size of a walnut. Dip into melted margarine. Roll in a mixture of sugar, cinnamon and finely chopped nuts. Gently place in greased tube or bundt pan. Let rise until doubled, about 45 minutes. Bake 35-40 minutes at 375°.

Dinner Rolls

Cut dough into 32 equal pieces. Shape into balls. Place in two 9" x 12" greased baking pans. Let rise until doubled, about 45 minutes. Bake 20-25 minutes at 400°.

ORANGE ROLLS

These have become a Saturday tradition on the Anderson farm. The boys always manage to come in from the fields just as the rolls come out of the oven.

2 packages dry yeast
1/2 cup warm water

3/4 cup margarine
1/3 cup sugar
6 eggs

1 cup milk, heated to lukewarm
1/2 tsp. salt

4 cups stone ground flour
4 - 4 1/2 cups all-purpose flour

1/4 cup margarine, softened
3/4 cup brown sugar
Grated rind of 1 orange
1 Tbsp. cinnamon

3 cups powdered sugar
4 Tbsp. orange juice

Dissolve yeast in water. Cream margarine and sugar. Beat in eggs, one at a time. Stir in yeast, milk and salt. Stir in stone ground flour. Gradually add enough of the all-purpose flour to make a soft dough.

Turn dough out onto lightly floured board and knead until smooth and elastic, about 5 minutes. Place dough in greased bowl, turn once to grease top, cover with a towel and let rise in a warm place until doubled, about 45 minutes.

Turn onto lightly floured board and punch down. Knead 2 minutes. Roll into a rectangle 18" x 9". Brush on 1/4 cup softened margarine. Sprinkle with brown sugar, grated rind of 1 orange and cinnamon. Pat down well with hands so that the mxture sticks to the margarine. Roll up, beginning at the wide side. Pinch to seal.

Cut with a serrated knife into 3/4-inch slices. Put into 3 greased 9" cake pans or two 8" x 12" pans. Bake 20 minutes at 374°.

While warm, frost with powdered sugar and orange juice mixed until smooth.

VEGETABLES AND MAIN DISHES

ZUCCHINI PANCAKES

1/3 cup stone ground flour
1/2 tsp. baking powder
1/2 tsp. salt
1/4 cup grated Parmesan cheese
Dash pepper

2 eggs, slightly beaten
2 medium zucchini, shredded (about 2 cups)

2 Tbsp. margarine

Blend together dry ingredients. Stir in eggs and zucchini.

Melt margarine in frying pan. Drop about 2 Tbsp. batter into hot pan. Bake 2 or 3 minutes; turn and bake another 2 minutes. Makes 12 cakes.

EASY POTATO PANCAKES

3 eggs

1/4 cup milk
1/3 cup stone ground flour
1 tsp. salt
1/8 tsp. nutmeg

1 package (12-oz.) frozen shredded hash brown potatoes, thawed
1/2 cup frozen chopped onions, thawed

Beat eggs well. Add milk, flour, salt and nutmeg to the eggs and beat until smooth. Stir in hash browns and onions.

Grease heated griddle. Pour on 1/4 cup batter for each cake. Flatten gently. Fry about 2 minutes on each side.

Keep warm in 150° oven until ready to serve. Makes 12 pancakes.

CREAMED CARROTS

8 carrots, scrubbed and sliced

2 Tbsp. butter or margarine
2 Tbsp. stone ground flour
1/4 tsp. salt

1 cup milk

1 tsp. sugar
1/8 tsp. nutmeg

Boil or steam carrots just until tender. Drain, reserving liquid.

Meanwhile, melt butter or margarine over low heat. Blend in flour and salt. Gradually stir in milk. Bring to a boil and boil 1 minute, stirring constantly. Stir in sugar and nutmeg. Blend in drained liquid to desired consistency.

Add carrots to sauce. Simmer gently for 5 minutes, stirring frequently.

POTATO DUMPLINGS
(Kartoffelklösse)

These are fun to make and go well with roast beef. Try them for a change from mashed or boiled potatoes.

4 medium potatoes

2 Tbsp. butter
1 tsp. salt
Dash nutmeg

1 egg, beaten
1 cup stone ground flour

1/2 cup butter, melted
1/2 cup bread crumbs

Boil unpeeled potatoes until tender. Peel and put through ricer (or grate coarsely). Stir in butter, salt and nutmeg. Chill.

Blend egg into chilled potatoes. Add enough flour (about 1/2 cup) to make mixture easy to handle. Form into 1" balls and roll in remaining flour.

Drop half the potato balls gently into boiling, salted water. Cook uncovered 10 minutes. Remove with slotted spoon and drop into shallow bowl with melted butter. Roll to coat evenly. Keep in warm oven while cooking remaining dumplings.

Sprinkle with bread crumbs before serving.

SPINACH CHEESE CASSEROLE

3 eggs
1/3 cup stone ground flour
1/2 lb. Cheddar cheese, grated
2 cups cottage cheese
1 tsp. salt

2 packages (10 oz. each) frozen spinach, thawed and drained

Beat together eggs, flour, cheeses and salt until smooth. Add spinach and blend well.

Pour into greased 8" x 12" pan. Bake 45 minutes at 350°.

SAUTEED FISH FILLETS

1/2 cup stone ground flour
1/4 tsp. salt
Dash pepper

2 lbs. fish fillets

Stir salt and pepper into flour with a fork to blend well.

Dip fish in flour and saute in hot oil in skillet 2 to 3 minutes on each side.

Serve with lemon wedges.

Stone ground flour is excellent for coating or breading meats and vegetables — good flavor and texture.

BAKED CHICKEN

1 cup stone ground flour
1/2 cup Parmesan cheese, grated
1/4 cup minced dried parsley
1 tsp. salt
1/8 tsp. pepper
1 tsp paprika

1 chicken, cut up -- or pieces totaling about 3 1/2 lbs.
1/2 cup margarine, melted

Stir together dry ingredients in a bowl. Dip chicken pieces in margarine, then in flour mixture. Arrange in a shallow baking pan. Bake for 45 minutes at 375º.

To cut calories, remove skin and fat from chicken and substitute buttermilk for margarine.

OVEN-FRIED CHICKEN

1/2 cup stone ground flour
1 tsp. salt
1/2 tsp. paprika
1/2 tsp. nutmeg
1/4 tsp. pepper

2 1/2 - 3 lbs. chicken pieces

1/4 cup cooking oil
2 Tbsp. margarine

Mix flour, salt, paprika, nutmeg and pepper in a plastic bag. Add chicken pieces 2 at a time and shake well.

Place baking pan or cast iron skillet with oil and margarine in oven and heat to 400º. Place coated chicken pieces skin side down in the pan. Bake uncovered 30 minutes. Turn chicken and bake 20 minutes longer, or until chicken is done.

RUNZA

These versatile meat and cabbage-filled rolls are perfect for a casual supper in front of the fireplace. They freeze well for a quick lunch, too. Thaw 20 minutes in oven or 1 minute for each Runza in the microwave oven.

2 cups warm water
2 packages dry yeast
1/4 cup sugar
1 1/2 tsp. salt

1 egg
1/4 cup margarine, softened
3 cups stone ground flour
3 1/2 - 4 cups all-purpose flour

Mix water, yeast, sugar and salt until dissolved. Add egg and margarine. Stir in flour. Knead a few minutes to make a smooth dough. Refrigerate 4 hours.

Roll dough into oblong shape and cut into 24 squares. Roll or pat each piece to about 4 to 5 inch square. Place 3-4 Tbsp. cold hamburger mixture on each square. Pull corners together, apple dumpling style, and pinch together tightly. Place on greased cookie sheets. Bake 20 minutes at 350°. Serve hot or cold.

Hamburger mixture:

1 1/2 lbs. hamburger
1/2 cup chopped onion
3 cups shredded cabbage
1/4 cup water
1 1/2 tsp. salt
1/2 tsp. pepper
Dash Tabasco

Brown hamburger and onion. Pour off excess grease. Add cabbage, water and seasonings. Simmer 15-20 minutes. Cool completely before wrapping in dough.

COOKIES

CHOCOLATE CHIP OATMEAL COOKIES

2 cups stone ground flour
1 1/2 cups quick rolled oats
1 tsp. soda
1 tsp. salt

1 cup shortening or margarine
1 cup white sugar
1/2 cup brown sugar
1 tsp. vanilla

2 eggs

1 package (12 oz.) chocolate chips

Mix together flour, oats, soda and salt. Cream margarine, sugars and vanilla. Beat in eggs. Add flour mixture and blend well. Stir in chocolate chips.

Drop by rounded teaspoons onto greased cookie sheets. Bake 10-12 minutes at 350°.

LINDA'S SPICY SNICKERDOODLES

1 cup shortening
1 1/2 cups sugar
1 tsp. vanilla

2 eggs

2 1/4 cups stone ground flour
2 tsp. cream of tartar
1 tsp. soda
1 tsp. cloves
1/2 tsp. salt

Cream together shortening, sugar and vanilla. Beat in eggs. Sift together dry ingredients and add to creamed mixture.

Roll into balls, then roll balls in a mixture of 3 Tbsp. sugar, 1 tsp. cinnamon and 1 Tbsp. finely ground nuts. Place on cookie sheet and bake 12-15 minutes at 375°.

LEMON SQUARES

1/2 cup all-purpose flour
1/2 cup stone ground flour
1/4 cup powdered sugar
1/2 cup margarine

Measure dry ingredients into a bowl. Stir with a fork to blend. Mix in margarine and press into an 8" x 8" pan. Bake 15 minutes at 350°.

Beat together:

2 eggs
1 cup granulated sugar
1/2 tsp. baking powder
3 Tbsp. lemon juice

Pour over the baked crust, return to oven and bake 20-25 minutes at 350°. Cool, dust with powdered sugar and cut into squares.

BANANA BUTTERSCOTCH SQUARES

A good way to use up that ripe banana.

1 2/3 cups stone ground flour
1 1/2 tsp. baking powder
1/2 tsp. salt

1/3 cup margarine
1 1/4 cups brown sugar

1 egg, slightly beaten
1 ripe banana, mashed

1/2 tsp. vanilla
1/2 cup chopped walnuts
1 package (6 oz.) butterscotch chips

Measure dry ingredients into bowl. Stir through with a fork to blend.

Cream margarine and sugar. Beat in egg and banana. gradually beat in dry ingredients and vanilla. Add walnuts and butterscotch chips and blend well.

Spoon into 8" x 12" greased pan. Bake 30 minutes at 350°. Cut into squares while warm.

GLAZED DATE-NUT BARS

These unusual bars are delicious -- firm and chewy.

1 cup stone ground flour
1 cup all-purpose flour
1/2 tsp. salt

3/4 cup soft margarine
1 cup brown sugar
3 eggs
1 tsp. vanilla

1 cup shredded coconut
1 cup chopped filberts or walnuts
1 cup chopped dates

Stir together flours and salt.

Cream margarine and sugar. Beat in eggs and vanilla. Add flour mixture. Stir in coconut, nuts and dates.

Spread batter in well-greased 9" x 13" pan. Drizzle hot glaze over batter. Bake 30 minutes at 350°. Cut into bars.

GLAZE

3/4 cup brown sugar
3 Tbsp. light cream
1 1/2 Tbsp. margarine

Stir together brown sugar, cream and margarine in small saucepan. Boil over medium heat for 1 minute.

CAKES

CHOCOLATE SHEET CAKE

This is one of those special recipes that is passed from friend to friend, which we have adapted for use with stone ground flour.

2 cups stone ground flour
2 cups sugar
1/2 tsp. salt

1 cup water
1/2 cup margarine
1/2 cup oil
1/4 cup cocoa

1/2 cup buttermilk
1 tsp. soda
2 eggs
1 tsp. vanilla

Combine first three ingredients in a mixer bowl. Combine water, margarine, oil and cocoa in a saucepan and bring to a boil. Add to flour mixture and mix well. Beat in buttermilk, soda, eggs and vanilla.

Pour into greased and floured jelly roll pan. Bake 20 minutes at 400°. Spread frosting on while hot. When cooled, cut into squares.

FROSTING

1/4 cup margarine
2 Tbsp. cocoa
3 Tbsp. milk

2 cups powdered sugar
1/2 cup ground nuts (optional)
1/2 tsp. vanilla

Place margarine, cocoa and milk in a pan and bring to a boil. Stir in powdered sugar, nuts and vanilla.

CARROT-APPLESAUCE BUNDT CAKE

3/4 cup margarine
2 cups brown sugar, firmly packed
2 eggs

2 cups stone ground flour
2 cups all-purpose flour
1 Tbsp. soda
2 tsp. cinnamon
2 tsp. nutmeg

2 cups applesauce
1 1/2 cups shredded raw carrots

1 1/2 cups chopped walnuts

Cream margarine and sugar. Beat in eggs. Measure dry ingredients into a bowl and stir with a fork to blend.

Gradually add dry ingredients alternately with applesauce and carrots to margarine and sugar. Fold in nuts.

Pour into greased and floured Bundt pan or 10" tube pan. Bake at 350° for 1 hour and 20 minutes or until firm. Cool in pan 5 minutes.

Turn out onto rack. Sprinkle with powdered sugar. Cool before slicing.

Bundt cakes decorate beautifully for a special gift for any season.

GINGERBREAD

Serve warm with cider sauce, applesauce, whipped cream or plain.

1 1/2 cups stone ground flour
1 Tbsp. baking powder
2 tsp. ginger
1 1/2 tsp. cinnamon
1/2 tsp. salt

1 egg
1/3 cup sugar
1/3 cup oil
2/3 cup molasses
3/4 cup buttermilk

Measure dry ingredients into a bowl. Mix well with a fork.

In large electric mixer bowl beat together remaining ingredients until smooth. Slowly beat in dry ingredients just until blended.

Pour into well-greased 8" x 8" pan. Bake 45 minutes at 350°.

CIDER SAUCE

2 Tbsp. butter or margarine
2 Tbsp. cornstarch
1 1/4 cups apple cider
1/2 cup brown sugar, loosely packed

Melt butter or margarine in small saucepan. Blend in cornstarch. Stir in cider and brown sugar and cook until thick and clear. Serve warm over gingerbread.

APPLESAUCE HONEY CUPCAKES

1 1/4 cups stone ground flour
1 cup all-purpose flour
1 tsp. cinnamon
1/2 tsp. nutmeg
1/2 tsp. ground ginger
1/2 tsp. salt
1 tsp. soda

1/2 cup soft margarine
1 cup honey
1 egg
1 tsp. vanilla

1 cup applesauce

Measure dry ingredients into a bowl. Mix well with a fork.

In a large mixer bowl, beat together margarine and honey. Beat in egg and vanilla. Gradually add applesauce and dry ingredients alternately to the honey mixture.

Spoon into paper-lined muffin tins. Bake 30 minutes at 350°. Makes 2 dozen cupcakes.

PIES AND DESSERTS

PIE CRUST

This crust complements our favorite berry filling on the following page.

1 cup stone ground flour
1 cup all-purpose flour
1 tsp. salt

3/4 cup shortening

4-5 Tbsp. cold water

Stir together flours and salt. Cut in shortening. Sprinkle water over mixture and stir lightly until evenly moistened. Form into 2 balls with hands. Roll out on lightly floured pastry cloth. Makes one 2-crust pie or two 1-crust pies.

To bake 1-crust pie shell without filling, arrange crust in pan, flute edge, prick bottom and sides of shell with a fork, and bake at 425° for 15 minutes.

Keep a shaker of cinnamon-sugar on hand for sprinkling on crusts. Use 1 teaspoon cinnamon for each 1/4 cup sugar.

BERRY PIE

Grandma Dietz's wild blackberry pie. Berries were always picked at their peak of ripeness from our favorite patch by the creek. The ripe berries don't require as much sugar, but a little more of the tapioca for thickening. Any of the cane berries or blueberries may be used in this recipe. Adjust sugar and tapioca to the sweetness and juiciness of the berry.

Pastry for 9" 2-crust pie
1 quart fresh berries

3/4 - 1 cup sugar
4 Tbsp. minute tapioca
1/2 - 1 tsp. cinnamon

1 Tbsp. butter or margarine

Arrange berries in pastry-lined pie pan. Stir together sugar, tapioca and cinnamon. Spoon evenly over berries, tapping pan to distribute sugar evenly through berries. Dot with butter or margarine.

Cover with top crust, sealing edges to retain juices. Make several slits in top to let steam escape. Sprinkle crust with a cinnamon-sugar mixture. Bake at 425° for 35-45 minutes, or until crust is golden.

For thickening pie, stone ground flour works beautifully in place of the tapioca.

APPLE CRISP

When apples are plentiful, this is an easy way to use them for dessert.

4 cups peeled, sliced apples

2/3 cup brown sugar
1/2 cup stone ground flour
2/3 cup oatmeal

1/2 tsp. cinnamon
1/2 tsp. nutmeg
1/4 cup margarine, melted

Put apples in buttered baking dish. Blend remaining ingredients together until crumbly. Sprinkle on top of apples. Bake 30 minutes at 375°. This bakes nicely in the microwave; bake 20 minutes, turning once during baking.

Serve warm with ice cream or whipped cream.

When we have access to surplus apples, we peel and slice and freeze them in quart containers. We also keep extra batches of the topping in the freezer. When we need a quick dessert, we simply empty a quart of partially thawed apples into a baking dish, sprinkle the thawed topping mix on the apples and place it in the oven.

PEAR STREUSEL DESSERT

4 cups sliced pears (about 4 large pears)
3 Tbsp. sugar
3 Tbsp. stone ground flour

1 cup stone ground flour
1/2 cup finely chopped walnuts
1/2 cup sugar
1 tsp. cinnamon
1/4 cup margarine, softened

Peel and slice pears. Gently stir in 3 Tbsp. sugar and 3 Tbsp. flour. Place in greased 8" x 8" baking dish.

Blend flour, walnuts, sugar, cinnamon and margarine with pastry blender or fork. Spread over pears. Bake 35 minutes at 350°.

Serve with whipped topping.

STONE-CRACKED
WHEAT CEREAL

So many of our friends have been such enthusiastic users of cracked wheat for cereal that we had to give it a try. What we discovered was not only a very tasty and satisfying cereal, but also one which is easy to prepare.

Marcie's Method:

1 cup cracked wheat
4 cups water
1/2 tsp. salt

Place wheat, water and salt in top of double boiler. Cover and place over bottom of double boiler in which water is gently simmering. Cook 1 hour.

You can start this the night before. Cook for about 45 minutes. Turn heat off and let it sit overnight. In the morning turn heat on again and reheat for about 30 minutes. Makes 3-4 servings.

Store left-over cereal in refrigerator. Reheat in double boiler 30 minutes. Reheats nicely in a microwave oven.

Arlene's Method:

1 cup cracked wheat
1/2 tsp. salt
3 cups boiling water

Stir cracked wheat and salt into boiling water in a heavy pan such as cast aluminum. Simmer approximately 25 minutes, stirring once or twice. Makes 2-3 servings.

This cereal is very good served just with warm milk. For those who prefer sweetening, add a little honey or sugar.

INDEX